Our Gift to t...

M000032479

Margarita González-Jensen

Photographs by Richard Hutchings

Rigby

A Harcourt Achieve Imprint

www.Rigby.com

1-800-531-5015

Mom and I went to the beach.

We looked at the beach.
The beach was messy.

We wanted to help
the beach.

Mom picked up a can.
I picked up paper.

We picked up cups.
We picked up bags, too.

The beach was clean.
Mom and I were happy.

I found pretty shells.

I picked up the shells.

I found wood.

I picked up the wood.

I found rocks, too.
I picked up the rocks.

I helped the beach,
and I had fun!